mixed media:
new studio techniques

ISOBEL HALL & MAGGIE GREY

Contents

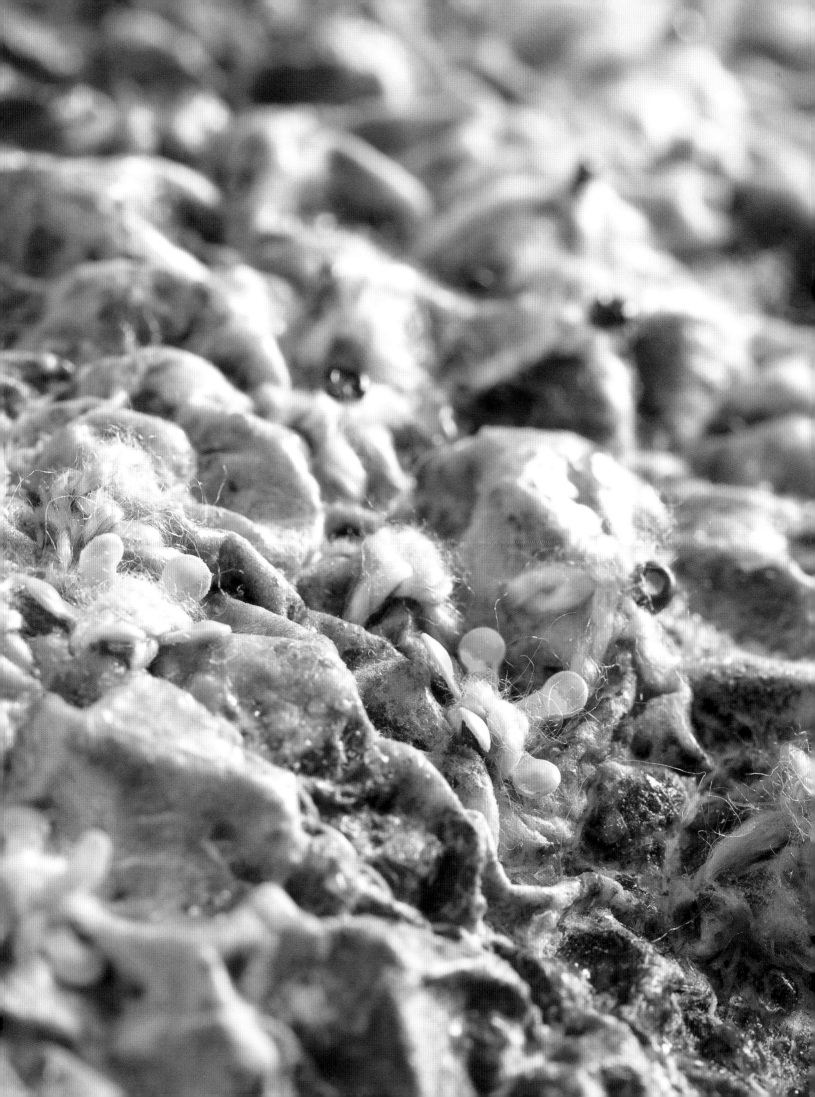

Introduction

This book began life as one about personal wearable art – textile jewellery and accessories – but, on the way, it insisted on exploring diversions such as wall panels and three-dimensional art. So we let it have its way and enjoyed the ride.

We also decided that the book would be a real teaching aid with clear step-by-step photos that encourage you to get a good grasp of basic techniques before trying our suggestions for ways of extending them – going beyond the basics.

The wonderful thing about working with fabrics, stitch and mixed media is that there is rarely a right or wrong way to do things. A flexible approach is often the best. Sometimes the back can look better than the front, so keep turning your work over to evaluate it.

Always exercise caution when using heat with powders, waxes and flammable fabrics. Work in a well-ventilated area and consider wearing a mask or respirator.

Mixed media can be expensive but, with careful thought, a lot of money can be saved by using everyday things that are around us, and we have a whole chapter suggesting ways to do this. Charity shops or 'free-cycle' websites are often good places to find jewellery items which you can cannibalise or use as a base. They also have interesting pieces of equipment which can have a new life in making art. Keep all off-cuts from fabrics and papers as these can build up into a glorious new piece.

> Bangles with wire or plastic as a base.

CHAPTER I

MATERIALS

Most of the materials we use are easily obtainable by mail order. We've experimented with a variety of media in this book but it is not necessary to buy all of them and many of the papers are very inexpensive. Your own stash of paints will be useful and will save money. The recycling section should make use of lots of completely free materials.

The early chapters deal with the technique of laminating layers of paper – an exciting process with many creative options. Papers that have been painted, stamped or inkjet-printed can all be layered and included in your work – great for incorporating text seamlessly into a textile. The technique is based on layering fine papers such as tissue, bookbinder's tissue or teabag paper over a base of painted paper or fabric. An acrylic medium is used to bond the fragile papers to the surface and this has the advantage of making the papers transparent. Whichever paper you use, you will find that outlines laminated over a pale surface work best – text is great.

Later chapters show how encaustic wax and embossing powder could add another dimension to your work. Oiled paper is also huge fun and provides an amazing surface for stitch. This technique requires a slightly heavier paper and gives a great texture.

Sealants

Sealing papers and fabrics, using any of the following products, will change them dramatically. All of them make a contribution to stiffening the fabric. Sometimes this is desirable but it will certainly inhibit any draping characteristics. Good all-purpose sealants are Ormoline fabric medium or acrylic wax. The former gives a matt appearance and the latter leaves a gloss. Both remain easy to stitch.

You could also use Jo Sonja's sealer, diluted PVA or one of the Mod Podge sealers. Our least favourite is diluted PVA as it is difficult to stitch. Mod Podge sealers can be bought in many varieties, the most obvious being matt, satin or gloss. This sealer is cheaper than many others but it does leave a plasticised appearance. It works well over thin fragile papers such as bookbinder's repair tissue or teabag paper and it can later be stitched by hand or machine. Simply use a paintbrush to paint the sealant of your choice over the fabric or paper. Using a sealant to bond thin porous papers to a base fabric is simple and produces interesting effects. Try Sparkle Mod Podge or Shimmer for different mixed media effects.

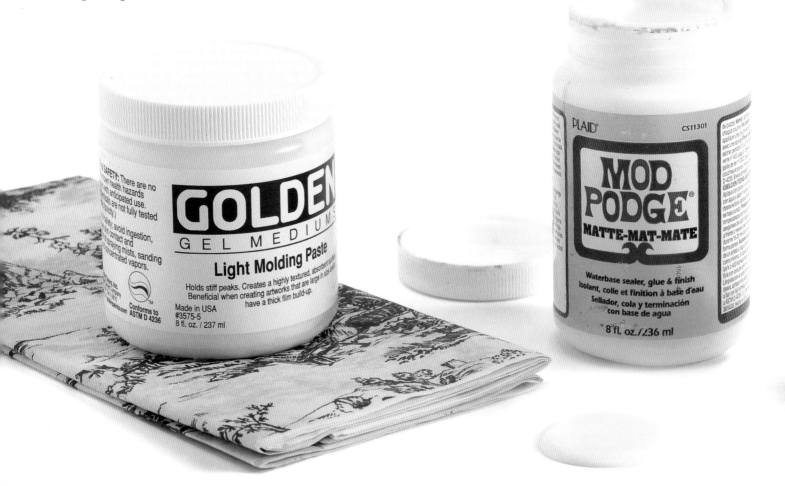

Paper

Tissue paper is often used to provide a textured appearance but it can sometimes lead to an unacceptable shine. Teabag paper is often a better option as it becomes totally translucent without any shine. Bookbinder's tissue can be hard to find but it is very strong – useful where the item may experience a lot of use. Ordinary tissue paper can be used but be aware that the shiny back can inhibit the sealant. In this case, paint the background with sealant first before applying the tissue. Commercially printed tissue paper can be fun to use, especially if it has some fancy text.

Thin porous papers will not stand proud on the fabric so, if you want the design element on the paper to stand out, you must bond it to a paper or fabric that has a white or pale-coloured background.

Alternatively, you can bond it to a fabric that has a more pronounced coloured background and the design will almost disappear, leaving a fabric with added interest and haphazard pattern.

The one rule we offer is to stop when you get to a stage where you like what you see. Do not go on to add further experimentation as the process will be irreversible. Instead, work a sample page in a sketchbook, using the same materials as the 'big' piece. Then you can try any way-out experiments on that page to see how they work.

> Sketchbook with folded insert showing a variety of lamination techniques.

CHAPTER 2

SEALANTS, WAXES AND OILS

The process of lamination is a simple one and there's lots of fun to be had in experimenting. It's always best to start simple and build up, so here is a method for a wall panel, first the background and then a suggestion for a focal point.

Our inspiration for this piece was a faded fresco of 'The Three Graces'. It's best to have a rough idea of your design before you start.

∧ Sketchbook design including a drawing of 'The Three Graces' with laminated lettering.

YOU'LL NEED:

- Piece of heavyweight paper
- Spray paint
- Gold and one colour in acrylic paint
- FuseFX (Gossamer Fuse)
- Teabag paper
- Stamp

HERE'S HOW:

STEP 1

Paint or spray a background paper. This is fairly thick sketchbook (cartridge) paper, sprayed with Moonshadow Mist paint. Watercolour or Adirondack spray paints could be used for a more colourful effect but don't make the colour too dark. After spraying, and while the paint is still wet, use a paintbrush to smooth some areas.

STEP 2

FuseFX (Gossamer Fuse) in black is then ironed over the top. Use baking paper on the ironing surface and over the FuseFX. Do make sure that you are only ironing one layer of the fusible webbing. For more texture a little gold acrylic paint can be added in some places over the top of the FuseFX.

STEP 3

While this is drying, stamp some teabag paper using acrylic paint. Spread the paint thinly onto baking paper and place the stamp on top.

You could also use a stamp pad – the paint and ink give very different results when laminated onto the background, which adds interest if the same stamp is used. Some lettering could also be stamped with a pad.

STEP 4

When dry, tear the stamped teabag paper into strips and lay on the background and begin the lamination process. For the piece shown here, Jo Sonja's sealant was used over the top of each strip to laminate it and stick it down.

CONTINUED NEXT PAGE ▶

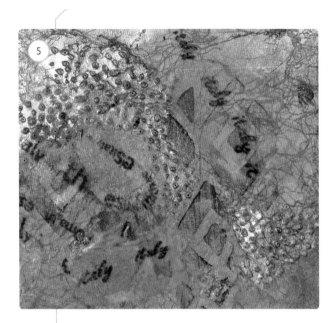

STEP 5

When all is dry, spray adhesive over the back of the paper and stick it to a light backing fabric, cut to size. Evolon is great for this purpose but thin cotton would work too. Try pushing a darning needle up from the back of the work to give added texture. This can be good to integrate any 'difficult' areas.

STEP 6

When this background was quite dry, a drawing was selected to become the top image. Our image was a drawing of figures from a fresco, which could be traced if you don't want to draw. Transfer the tracing to ordinary printer paper or any soft paper.

STEP 7

Colour the main areas, in this case the figures, with watercolour paints, Koh-i-Noor inks or similar, and crumple the paper when dry. Be careful not to tear it. Hold a pale-coloured pastel chalk flat over the surface and gently draw it over the highlights. An alternative could be an image torn from a magazine (be aware of copyright issues), a computer printout or a colour photocopy. Soft, inexpensive paper is best for this image.

STEP 8

Laminate the drawing to craft Vilene, Grungepaper (a firm compressed paper product) or similar. Use any of the products discussed earlier – Jo Sonja's was used here. When dry, stitch around the edges – just free machine straight stitching – and cut out the shapes.

STEP 9

Blend the edges by dipping a paintbrush in black ink (or any dark, runny paint) and colouring any white edges – don't worry if the ink spreads in a little, it adds definition. If you like the gilded look, a little gold wax – Treasure Gold or similar – can be applied lightly.

STEP 10

Lay the cut-out shape over the background and decide if any stitching is needed on the background to integrate the different areas. Working the figures first will avoid the need work areas that will be covered. Hand stitching was u but machining would work just as well.

STEP 11

Finally, apply the figures to the background. They could just be stuck with adhesive but it gives the piece a lift if they are raised slightly. A good way to do this is to cut a strip of metal from a soft-drinks can and fold it into three, lengthways, to give stability. Stick it to the figures with a strong glue, leaving some metal at either end. Bend upwards into an arc, fold the tabs back and stitch or glue them to the background.

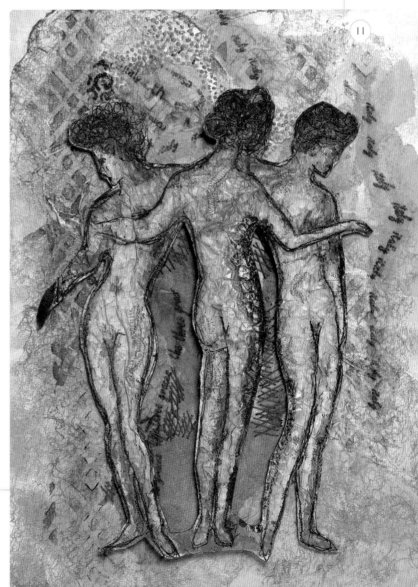

> The piece on the right shows the finished panel with the figures standing slightly proud of the background. Note the hand-stitching between the figures which integrates the shapes.

Grungepaper and stamped or printed paper

Grungepaper is a relative of Grungeboard but it is thinner with a smooth surface. Made of compressed paper, it is light and easy to stitch but firm enough for three-dimensional work such as vessels. Sealants can be used to laminate thin inkjet-printed papers to Grungepaper. Choose your design carefully – a strong colour on a pale background will show up well. In the box on the right we tell you how to print on teabag or tissue paper.

v Purchased ready-printed tissue paper can give a good effect. This one is laminated over a gesso and paint background. Although the colour is dark, it will not bleed in the same way as an inkjet-printed paper.

HERE'S HOW:

1. Cut freezer paper a little larger than the required size (I usually cut it to A4 size).
2. Place teabag paper over the shiny side of the freezer paper.
3. Cover with baking paper.
4. Iron over the sandwiched layers using a cool iron. If the iron is too hot or if you iron for a long period, the teabag paper will adhere to the freezer paper and it will be impossible to remove it. The teabag paper should be lightly adhered so that it can be removed at a later date.
5. I find it easier to tape the two papers to a carrier sheet with masking tape. Ensure that all of the paper is firmly adhered to the carrier sheet and that the four sides of the carrier sheet are protected with the tape.
6. Print on the teabag paper.
7. Remove the backing papers. The teabag paper should peel off easily. It will be very fragile.
8. Place the fragile printed teabag paper over the Grungepaper, which could be painted with gold acrylics to add a metallic sheen.
9. Adhere it to the Grungepaper by painting a sealant of your choice over the porous paper. Matt Mod Podge was used to bond the printed teabag paper to the Grungepaper illustrated here. Mod Podge dries very quickly, so about 15–30 minutes later it is possible to stitch into the Grungepaper by hand or machine.
10. If desired, holes can be punched in the Grungepaper. These do not necessarily need to be reinforced. Laces can be used to add interest.

TIP:

If there is too much black ink in your teabag print, it may bleed. Try to avoid images with heavy black lines and always leave your inkjet-prints for a day or two to 'cure' before using.

^ Printed teabag paper laminated to Grungepaper.

^ A small sample showing a variety of papers laminated to a
piece of Grungeboard. The papers include painted Japanese
paper and printed teabag paper.

Laminated paper over raised shapes

One of the joys of lamination is the fun of using very thin papers over a raised surface. You could use cut-out pieces of card or Grungeboard pre-cut shapes. Wallpaper with a raised pattern also works well and can be built up in layers on a base of paper or craft Vilene. Then cover with very fine painted papers, such as teabag or tissue. The best result – as with most lamination – comes with a pale wash of colour on the base and a dark linear design (stamp or printout) on the laminating paper. This could be tissue or teabag paper.

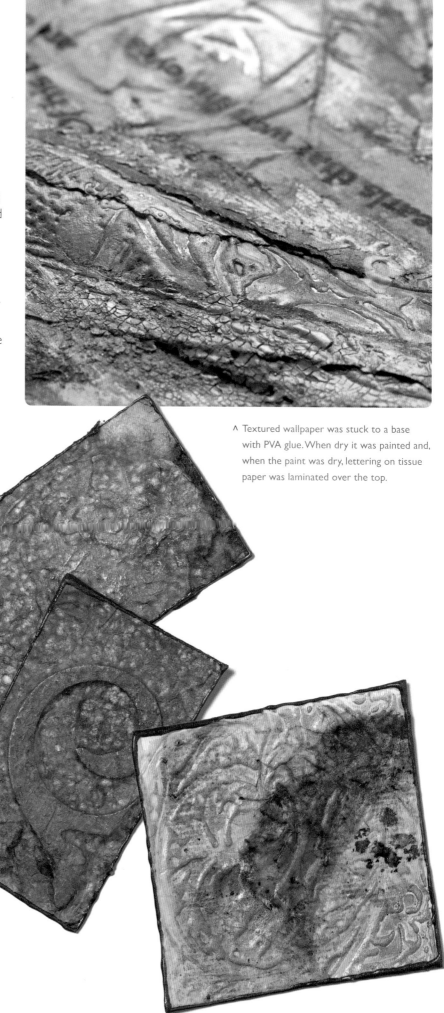

∧ Textured wallpaper was stuck to a base with PVA glue. When dry it was painted and, when the paint was dry, lettering on tissue paper was laminated over the top.

∧ Artists' Trading Cards and samples were made using Grungeboard shapes or wallpaper and a variety of painted papers.

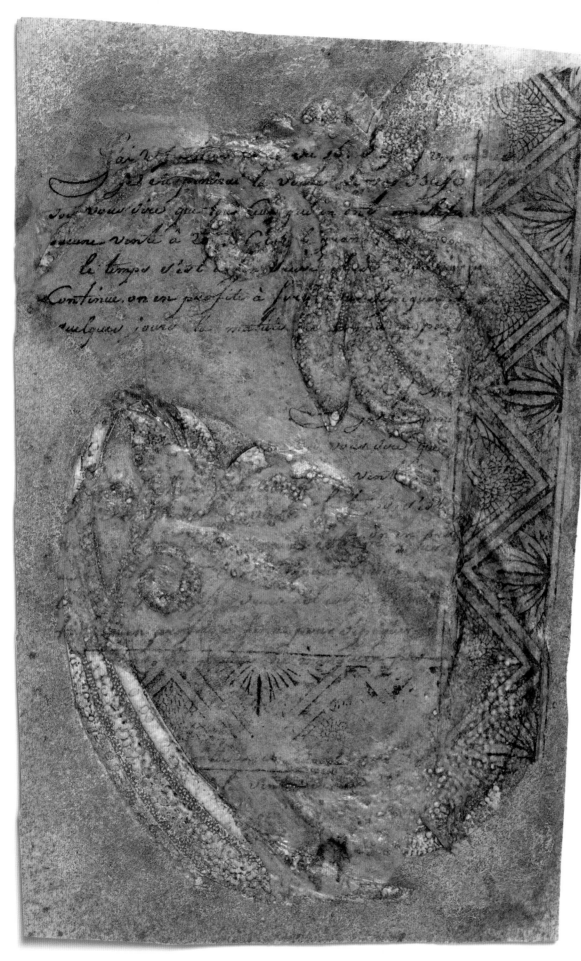

< Large motifs, cut from
  textured wallpaper, were
  laminated with tissue paper
  previously stamped using
  a lettering stamp. Borders
  were made by stamping
  the tissue with a patterned
  stamp. A good effect was
  obtained with the text
  appearing to rise out of
  the background shape.

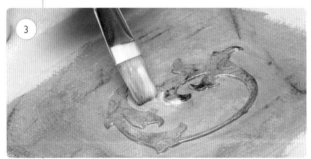

For high-relief shapes

HERE'S HOW:

STEP 1
Stick some Grungeboard shapes on card, Vilene or Grungepaper.

STEP 2
Paint or print some fine papers – teabag, fine tissue or Japanese papers work especially well. Here text is stamped on tissue paper.

STEP 3
As tissue is being used it is necessary to paint over the shapes with the medium.

STEP 4
Lay the paper on top of the shapes and press it into the medium. Start in the middle with an overlap of paper around the edges, as shown. Press really firmly to make the shape stand out.

STEP 5
Now laminate, as before, to make the tissue translucent.

STEP 6
When dry, use a very dry brush of gold acrylic paint to highlight the relief effect.

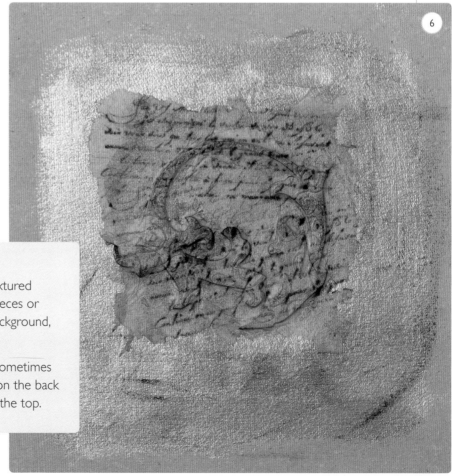

TIP:

Another good effect is to use laminated paper over textured wallpaper, as described on page 14. Simply stick torn pieces or motifs from the textured paper to a paper or fabric background, colour and then laminate.

Text works particularly well with raised shapes and is sometimes crisper on tissue paper. You may need to paint sealant on the back of the tissue before placing over the shape and sealing the top.

< 'Letter Box.' Letters were cut from Grungepaper and glued to a background. They were laminated using tissue paper and a lettering stamp. The background was cut to form four sides of a box and the edges joined by stitch before the strip (seen above) was glued to the box.

Fabric

Sheer fabric with Mod Podge

Most sealants dry clear but some, such as
Mod Podge, leave a film. This can be exploited,
especially with sheer fabric such as voile.

> Inkjet-printed teabag
paper, laminated to
voile with Mod Podge.

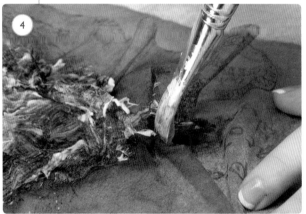

TRY THIS:

1. Rub chalky pastels into the voile.
   Blend a couple of colours – not too
   many or it will become muddy.
2. Shake off excess pastel and place
   the fabric on baking paper, crayoned
   side up. Baking paper is better for
   this technique than a non-stick mat
   which tends to dry shiny.
3. Liberally paint the Mod Podge over
   the fabric. It will seep through the
   fine fabric and pool on the back.
4. Nudge it a little with the end of a
   paintbrush to encourage little ridges.
5. Leave it to dry completely and then
   remove from the paper. Turn upside
   down and admire the back – a very
   distressed effect.
6. Use your favourite method
   to laminate a design onto the fabric.

> Furnishing voile after
colouring with pastels and
painting with Mod Podge.

∧ A very fine furnishing voile, such as this one with a lettering motif,
  is ideal for this technique.

^ > Printed teabag paper laminated onto sheer fabric
with acrylic wax for a long strip and a bangle.

Sheer fabrics with acrylic wax

Sheer fabrics can easily be laminated with thin papers. It is easy to stitch into this fabric as it is or it can be backed onto a stabiliser of your choice. Acrylic wax works well as a sealant for this technique as it does not leave a plasticised appearance.

HERE'S HOW:

1. Inkjet-print, stamp or paint your design on thin paper such as teabag paper, bookbinder's repair tissue or tissue paper.
2. Place baking paper on your work surface and lay the sheer fabric on this.
3. Position the decorated paper on the sheer fabric.
4. Paint acrylic wax over the thin paper. It will seep into the sheer fabric and, as it dries, it will bond the paper to the sheer.
5. When it is dry, remove it from the paper.

Sheer fabrics laminated in this way can be used for many things.

TIP:
LEFT-OVER FABRIC

1. Any left-over waxed silk fabric could be used to make a bracelet. First cut out the fabric to cover a brass bangle. To obtain the pattern size, spray 505 Spray glue onto the bangle. Cover it with paper. Draw around the outline. Remove the paper pattern and cut it out to size. Use this pattern piece to cut out the fabric to cover the bangle.
2. For the bangle above, milliner's netting was coloured, stitched in place and beaded.
3. Heat-moldable foam was twisted and heat set in position.
4. The twisted heat-moldable foam was painted and embroidered in running stitch. The braid can be stitched to the teabag paper fabric and bonded to the brass bangle using Copydex or other strong glue such as 'Incredibly Tacky' by Crafters' Pick.

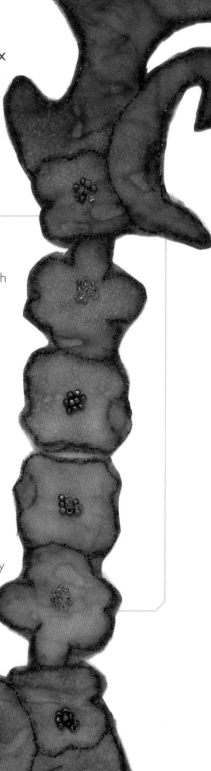

A design for a fresco panel was built up using a computer printout, laminated textured wallpaper and the Evolon and embossing enamel techniques described here. It acted as a trial for the panel opposite but works equally well as a stand-alone piece.

Painted Evolon with embossing powder

Evolon is a new microfilament fabric that you can paint, dye or print. As it does not fray, it will hold its shape when it is cut. It can be cut with a soldering iron and, of course, scissors. It feels like suede and is therefore tactile. As most mixed media techniques will affect the tactile qualities, this technique is more suitable for bags and bracelets than for scarves or wraps. Paint, stamp or marble this fabric and then try working on top of it. When it is dry, it can be worked on in a number of ways, as you can see in the detail below.

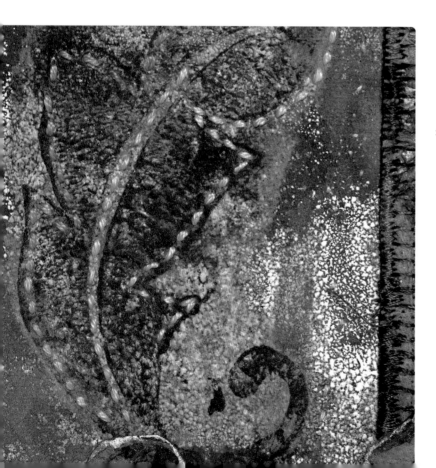

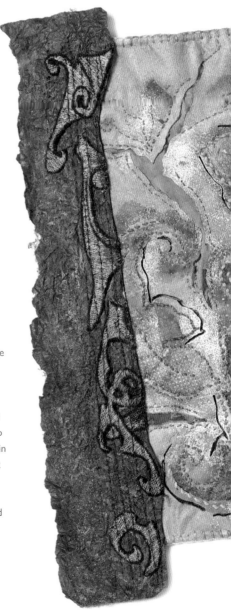

> The final panel that emerged from the trial pieces on this page was made by printing a fresco design onto Evolon (ironed onto freezer paper to print). A very small amount of water was splashed on with a paintbrush to make the colours run, resulting in an artful-looking angel in a track suit! Further panels were made from embossed Evolon placed over rust-dyed fabric and scored with a soldering iron to reveal the fabric below.

HERE'S HOW:

1. Paint over selected areas of the fabric with Ormoline medium.
2. Immediately sprinkle white opaque embossing powder over the fabric. Do not layer the powders thickly and do not overheat them.
3. Shake off the excess and heat using a heat tool.
4. Working outside and wearing a mask, attack the fabric with sandpaper or glasspaper to distress it.
5. Stamp, paint or inkjet-print your design onto thin paper such as bookbinder's tissue or teabag paper.
6. Now laminate the coloured Evolon by placing the paper over the top and painting with a sealant (Matt Mod Podge was used in the sample shown here). Parts of the design will show through the white areas underneath but other areas may be partially lost depending upon the depth of colour on the background.
7. Wait a little while for the paper to partially adhere. It is worth noting that Mod Podge dries very quickly and, once it has adhered, you will not be able to remove it. Use your finger to pull and scrape off small sections and thus distress it.
8. To make your design resemble medieval frescos, try embroidering an outline of a medieval architectural design.

Silk paper

We're quite sure that you've made silk paper before but we have some new ideas for it and they will be popping up throughout the book. There are lots of books on making the paper, so the basics will only be described briefly here before we move on to the fun part.

Silk fibres made into paper can result in a very robust fabric. Many different types of silk can be used. Our preferred choice is de-gummed silk filament. You can buy it ready dyed or in its natural state. You can use many different types of glue to bond the fibres – the best are Jo Sonja's, acrylic gloss medium and Ormoline. CMC paste or diluted PVA can also be used but CMC paste does tend to deteriorate over time and the resulting fabric is not as appealing. PVA is also less tactile and it is more difficult to stitch. Experiment to see which type of glue best suits your purpose.

Here are two ways to make silk paper – the first uses a medium and the second makes use of the natural gum in certain types of silk fibre.

∧ Bangle made from silk paper with machine-soluble lace.

> Silk paper strip bracelet with an embossed image.

Making the paper

A QUICK RECAP

1. Spread a net on a suitably protected area such as polythene sheeting.
2. Tease and pull out the fibres and lay them on the net.
3. Cover with another sheet of net.
4. Wet the fibres with a little washing-up liquid and water. Use the flat palm of your hands to push the liquid into the layers so that all of the fibres are wet. The washing-up liquid makes the fibres more receptive to the medium.
5. Mix one teaspoon of acrylic gloss medium with four teaspoons of water and brush it on the net. Use the flat palms of your hands to push this solution into the fibres. Turn the sandwiched layers over and repeat to ensure that the solution has penetrated all the layers.
6. Hang up the dripping layers to dry.
7. Place the sandwiched layers on a flat base and remove the net, one layer at a time.
8. The silk paper should now be ironed if you want a flat fabric. For a textured surface, leave it as it is.

You could also use cocoon strippings and omit the gloss medium. Just tease out the strippings onto baking paper and spray them with water. Cover with another layer and iron with a hot iron. They will stick together when dry. More layers can be built up on top of the base but the fabric will need to be painted with a sealant when dry.

∨ Clackerboard bangle: cocoon stripping paper laminated with printed teabag paper. Detail shown above.

Laminated and waxed papers for jewellery

Silk papers and paste fabric paper, see page 42, can be laminated in the same way that all the other surfaces are treated. The lamination may not show if the silk has bright colours so you could spread a little gesso over the area you wish to laminate. Teabag paper works well with silk, as does Lokta paper.

Print or draw your design on the paper and apply using your favourite medium. Then add stitching if desired. Do some samples with other papers as some of the 'hand-made' gift-wrap papers laminate well.

∧ A bangle made from paste fabric, laminated with printed teabag paper.

< Necklace formed from waxed cocoon stripping paper with stitched detail.

∧ Cocoon stripping paper bracelet which was laminated with printed teabag paper.

Silk paper with smocking thread

Great texture can be achieved by sewing with Madeira smocking thread or Grilon and then shrinking it with the steam from an iron. Madeira smocking thread was used to make the jewellery as it worked well on the robust silk paper.

∧ This ring has a felt base with silk paper, smocking thread and cotton-covered wire.

∧ Bracelet: silk paper and smocking threads with beaded details.

> Necklace: silk paper, smocking thread and cotton-covered wire make an attractive necklace.

Make the jewellery

HERE'S HOW:

1. Make robust silk paper by bonding the fibres using a solution of one teaspoon of acrylic gloss medium mixed with four teaspoons of water.
2. Use smocking thread and free machine embroidery to stitch shapes of your choice.
3. Activate the shrinking process by holding a steam iron over the silk paper. Do not iron directly on the paper.
4. Cut out the shapes.
5. To give more life to the pieces, try wire covered with sewing cotton around the edges. Invisible thread was used to sew the covered wire to the outside of the flowers.
6. Colour the paper and covered wire with paints of your choice. The jewellery was painted with red Twinkling H_2O paint.
7. Melt encaustic wax on an iron and iron it over the raised surfaces (we used burgundy and gold wax).
8. To seal the pieces, paint acrylic wax or Mod Podge over them. We used gloss Mod Podge here.

Blending encaustic waxes

Sometimes it is desirable to blend waxes to create another colour. Simply ironing the wax directly onto the fabric and then ironing a second colour over it can be unsightly. In order to be completely in control of the amount of wax that is transferred and to obtain a uniform colour combination, try the method described here. In this instance we are transferring wax to the raised surfaces of crushed silk.

TRY THIS:
1. Iron the first colour directly onto baking paper.
2. Iron the second colour over the wax on the baking paper.
3. Blend the two colours by ironing over the waxed paper.
4. Place the waxed paper face down over the fabric.
5. Transfer the blended waxes onto the raised surfaces by lightly ironing and then quickly removing the paper. Keep peeking to ensure an even application.

The residue of wax on the baking paper can be re-used on other projects. The wax will solidify on the paper and will flake off in lumps, so it needs to be stored with care. Try folding the paper for future use and, when you do re-open it, be aware that until you iron over it the wax pieces will not be attached to the non-stick paper.

> The scarf was fashioned from dyed crushed silk with blended encaustic waxes. It was then hand embroidered in Sorbello stitch.

> The bag matches the scarf and was made in a similar way. It has wrapped plastic handles.

< 'Duomo' bag. This was
made from faux chenille
with twisted Softsculpt
inserts. It was based on
a sketchbook drawing
of the columns at the
Duomo in Florence.

Blended wax with Softsculpt

This bag was worked with faux chenille, blended
waxes and strips of a material called Softsculpt.
This material, a thin foam, can be manipulated
into many shapes.

The bag is called *Duomo* because it is based
on marble architecture and features twisted
Softsculpt between the faux chenille tramlines.
The twisted Softsculpt represents twisted marble
columns – often seen in Gothic architecture.
The other embroidery between the tramlines is
twisted chain stitch. The colours used are based
on those on the Duomo in Florence.

Faux chenille

The faux chenille used to make the fabric for the bag is soft and tactile. It can be made into scarves, wraps, vests and jackets.

HERE'S HOW:

1. Select a minimum of three layers of fabric. The bottom fabric does not need to unravel at the edges but the others do. Consider colour values/contrast for all fabrics. The colour of the bottom fabric is the one that will show through when the top layers of fabric are cut.
2. Cut the layers of fabric into squares or rectangles.
3. Pin all of the layers together, with the non-fraying fabric on the bottom.
4. Sew straight parallel lines on the diagonal of the fabric about 1 cm (½in.) apart. Different widths will give different effects so it is worth experimenting first to see which you prefer.
5. Use sharp scissors to cut between the tramlines. Do not cut through the bottom layer.
6. Try withdrawing some of the threads or distressing the edges with the points of scissors. If the edges are not fluffy, put the fabric in a washing machine on its longest cycle and then pop it into the dryer.
7. Hand stitch between the tramlines or decorate as desired.

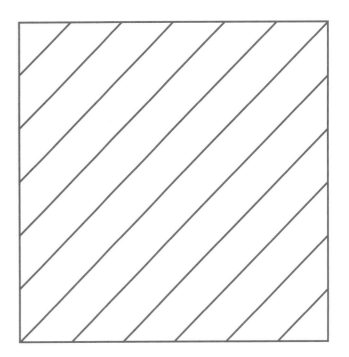

Making the bag

HERE'S HOW:

Silk fabric was used to make the faux chenille and silk carrier rods were ironed flat to make the supports for the stick handles. The Softsculpt was painted with encaustic wax.

1. Twist and set the Softsculpt strips. I do this by attaching the strip at one end to a corkboard with a drawing pin. Twist and secure the other end to the corkboard as before. Use a heat tool to twist and set the foam.
2. Melt the encaustic wax on the iron and iron it onto baking paper. Use more than one colour and blend the waxes on the baking paper by ironing over them.
3. Place the twisted strip onto the baking paper. Iron the wax to re-heat it but do not touch the Softsculpt. Quickly use a dedicated paintbrush to paint the Softsculpt.
4. Keep re-heating the wax on the paper. For the best effect, the foam should only be partially painted.

NOTE:

Do not re-heat the twisted Softsculpt or it will untwist. The wax **must** be applied by melting it and painting it on. Do not consider waxing the foam first and then twisting it. The reason for this is that the wax becomes toxic if overheated. Doing it as described above eliminates the risk of breathing in potentially toxic fumes.

> 'Monet's Garden'. Faux
chenille and twisted
Softsculpt, coloured with
encaustic wax.

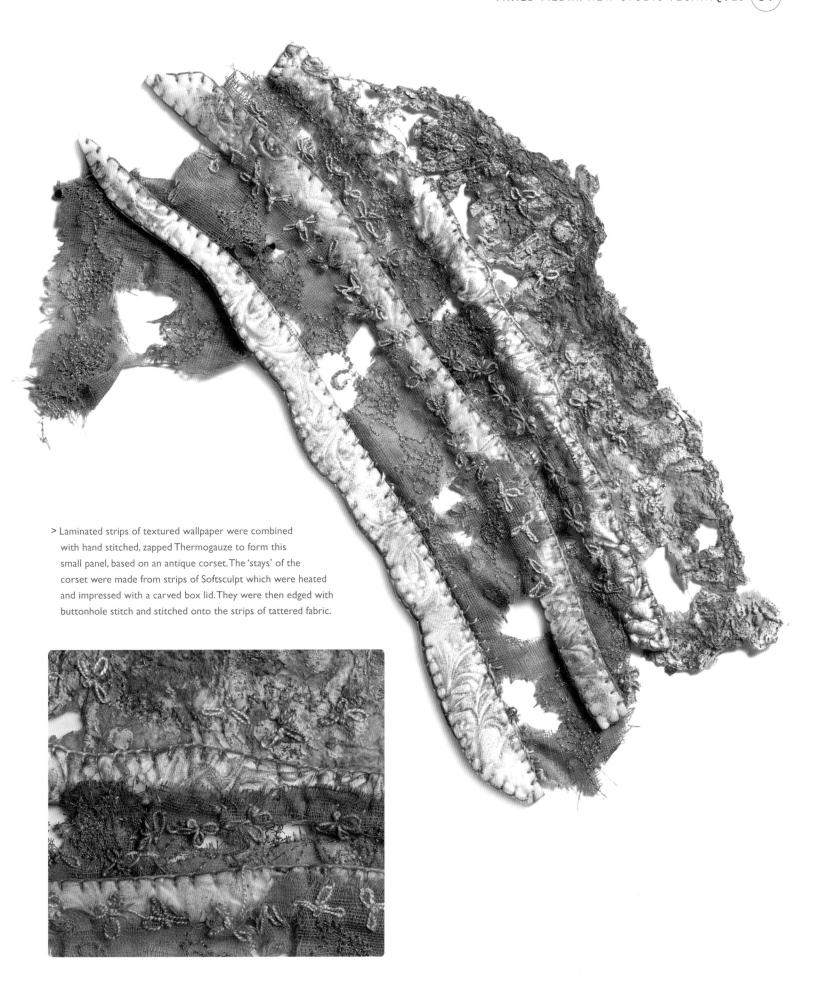

> Laminated strips of textured wallpaper were combined with hand stitched, zapped Thermogauze to form this small panel, based on an antique corset. The 'stays' of the corset were made from strips of Softsculpt which were heated and impressed with a carved box lid. They were then edged with buttonhole stitch and stitched onto the strips of tattered fabric.

Digital coatings

These are media for use on most porous surfaces, especially paper and card, which enable high-quality inkjet printing. However, they also give stunning paint effects – with no printer involved. Made by both Golden and inkAID, there are lots of different media to choose from, but we prefer the white matte version and this is used throughout the book. We have generally referred to the product as inkAID in our instructions. When the product is applied to foam stamps or painted through stencils, some strange but wonderful effects are obtained, especially if a metallic spray is combined with plain colour. All on cheap copy paper, too.

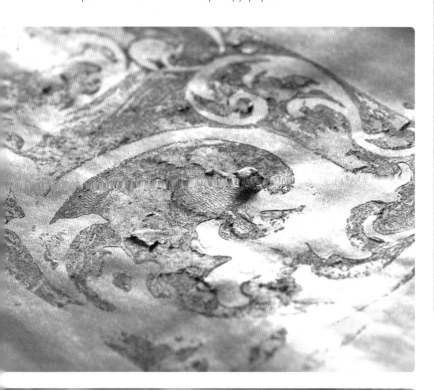

inkAID and paint

inkAID can be painted with a brush, dabbed with a sponge, printed with a foam stamp or through a stencil. It gives an interesting texture and is good to use over paper that has been painted or sprayed with a base colour.

HERE'S HOW:
1. Work on printer-weight paper and don't worry if it buckles.
2. Use a stencil (or, in the examples shown, the waste that remains after Grungeboard shapes have been removed) and dab the inkAID through with a sponge or brush. It can also be fun to paint all over the stencil with inkAID and press it down on the paper.
3. Allow it to dry and then use spray paints, either those bought for the purpose, or some inks or watercolours that you have decanted into spray bottles. Stick to two colours (orange and purple are shown here), leaving some areas unsprayed. Then spray a contrasting shade of Starburst Stain into the unpainted areas. This migrates in strange ways.
4. Dry completely and then crumple very gently in your hands, taking care not to tear the paper. Spray the back with a fabric adhesive and press onto felt.

Add hand or machine stitching.

< Plain copy paper was stencilled with inkAID, using a Grungeboard shape stencil. This is the stencil that remains when all the shapes have been removed. You can see in the photos here that the colour deepens in stencilled areas while the metallic paint is repelled by them.

> Some of the papers have been
bonded to felt or heavy interfacing,
stitched and then made into small books.
The attractive effect of the stencil or
stamped inkAID makes these items good
for the sales table at exhibitions.

Extensions

Other things to try:
- Make up a collage on the printer paper, using pieces of paper napkin, lacy paper, doilies and so on. Add colour and inkAID as above.
- Use firm paper – something like watercolour paper works well. These papers would be good in sketchbooks.
- Try it over a printout, highlighting some areas.

On page 36 we will look at oiling inkjet papers.

∧ This textured sample was made from scraps of cotton and torn pieces of scrim, all ironed onto freezer paper. It was painted with inkAID and printed on an inkjet printer. Some of the scrim adhered to the freezer paper, giving a very fragmented effect. Make sure when printing that the surface is not too bulky and that it is all secure. I keep a very cheap, simple printer for items of a bulky nature and would recommend this if you do a lot of printed experiments.

Inkjet printing

For general printing make sure that any fabric is secured to a backing:

1. Cut a piece of fine fabric and a piece of freezer paper, sized to go through the printer.
2. Iron fabric to paper. Paint the fabric with inkAID, not too heavily, and allow to dry thoroughly.
3. Print on 'best quality' setting. When dry remove from the backing.
4. Allow a day to set the ink, then add a felt backing and stitch.

FOR A SEMI-ABSTRACT EFFECT TRY THIS:

1. Print a colourful design on fine fabric, as above.
2. Print the same design on ordinary printer paper and immediately apply water to the printer paper to make the colours run.
3. When both are dry, crumple the paper to soften it.
4. Lay both pieces over a backing, such as felt, then tear the paper version and apply over the inkAID piece.
5. Stitch to meld the joins and apply to the backing.

This is very effective in loosening-up a piece, especially if you don't do abstracts – as you can see, right.

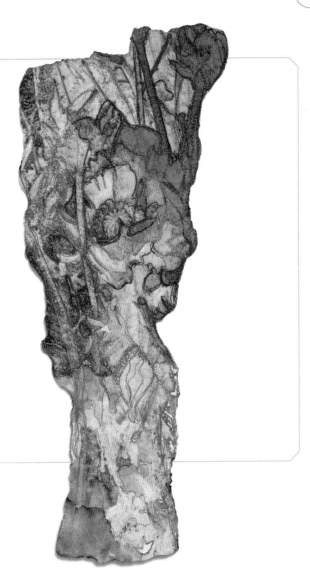

Black fabric

inkAID gives great results on black fabric – just fix to the freezer paper and then paint it in strips, or use a sponge, leaving gaps between, which will remain black. When printed, the colour will only be visible where painted with inkAID. Use fine fabric – polycotton is ideal.

< Fine black cotton was ironed onto freezer paper. It was then painted with inkAID in a streaky manner which meant that the colour only showed on the inkAID, not on the black fabric. In the piece on the left, more of this product was used to give vibrant colour. On the right, you can see how it was applied.

Oiled paper

Ordinary paper can achieve a very different look when oil is applied to it. Almost any oil will work, from almond oil to sunflower oil (as used in cooking). The trick is to work it into the paper with your hands – and this has the bonus effect of a beauty treatment for your skin at the same time. If using cooking oil, you might want to wash well afterwards.

For the basic technique, just take a piece of painted paper, not too stiff – we use everyday printer paper. Paint the paper with oil and then crumple it gently. Keep crumpling, folding and unfolding until the oil has penetrated the paper and it is soft and slightly shiny. Leave in a cool place to harden a little and then back with felt or a stabiliser and stitch. It does make a difference if you paint the front or the back – more on this later.

Try some options to jazz it up.

HERE'S HOW:
- Paint inkAID on printer paper and print before oiling.
- Use painted paper, crumple and then paint with black ink (or spray with a dark 'thin' paint) on the back.
- Oil before painting – use thin paint as before.
- Try a pale print or painting – the oil will make it almost translucent.

< This is a detail of the hanging shown on page 38. It shows the effect of the inkAID paper when it has been crumpled and oiled. The three small tribal figures were made from heavily machine-stitched felt which was painted with acrylic medium and covered with embossing powder which was then zapped with a heat tool.

> The Buddha was inspired by Chinese cave paintings. It was made by painting heavy Vilene with gesso, lightly sprayed with ink. When dry, it was laminated with ink drawings on tissue paper. When it was cut out, the tissue was wrapped over the cut edge and details added by machine embroidery. The printed, crumpled and oiled map shows the area of China in which the ancient cave paintings were found. Oiling light-coloured papers gives them an attractive translucent quality.

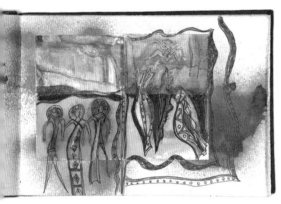

∧ This panel was inspired by a trip to Kakadu National Park in Australia's Northern Territory and the resulting sketchbook studies. Not having any art materials with me, I stamped some paper into the rich pigments of the soil and then drew with an ink pen. A small handbag printer (a Polaroid Pogo) was extremely useful and the prints were placed in the sketchbook and worked up by further drawing.

> 'Kakadu – beginnings'.
Wall panel based on a study of Aboriginal rock art. Permission was given to use the figures and imagery as I believe that this is important. Photographs and drawings were combined in printouts on inkAID paper which were then oiled and crumpled. After bonding to felt, hand and machine stitching completed the piece.

CHAPTER 3

LIGHT MOLDING PASTE

Molding pastes, made by Golden and Liquitex, are acrylic polymer emulsions which can be used to build up textured surfaces on fabrics.

Working on bought fabrics

Try experimenting with different types of fabrics and papers. On occasions, you may find that the fabric buckles if you use a thick, dense concentration of molding paste. This can be overcome by stretching the fabric in a frame and adding the paste while the fabric is taut. Leave the fabric in the frame until the paste is dry. Alternatively, fabrics such as cotton or calico can be ironed onto freezer paper prior to adding the paste. This backing paper should be left on until the paste is dry. The advantage of this technique is that you could inkjet-print the fabric prior to adding the paste. Whether you stretch the fabric you are working on or not will depend upon the weave.

Textured upholstery fabric with crackle paste

It's fun to combine Light Molding Paste with other materials. The bag, right, used it in combination with distress crackle paste and FuseFX (or Misty Fuse) to add texture to the surface. You will find more on crackle paste on page 56.

TRY THE FOLLOWING:

1. Furnishing fabric is robust, so lay it flat on the table for working. Use a spatula to spread the Light Molding Paste in designated areas.
2. Then paint other areas with a combination of Molding Paste and Old Peasant distress crackle paste.
3. When dry, use Twinkling H_2O paints over the surface of the two pastes.
4. Finally place two layers of white FuseFX over the fabric, cover with baking paper and iron.
5. The fabric is now ready to embroider.

> 'Spring Wedding' bag. Both molding and crackle pastes were used on furnishing fabric for this bag. The delicacy of the result shows what can be achieved with these basic materials.

Making molding paste fabric

Light Molding Paste can be used to make what we call a 'molding paste fabric'. This will be quite strong, easy to colour, stitch into and bead. Light Molding Paste by Golden has been used throughout this book. Be aware that you need Light Molding Paste for these techniques – other strengths and varieties will not work so well.

WARNING:

Do not leave molding paste fabrics on polished surfaces such as tables – they will mark. Always make a felt base for vessels that are made from molding paste.

It is best to work on baking Teflon as the thinner baking paper tends to ripple, and a Vaseline-greased baking tray is not supple enough to get the fabric off in one go.

TRY THIS:

1. Use a spatula to spread an even layer of Light Molding Paste on baking Teflon.
2. Leave it to dry. It may take a while, so patience is required. Do not be tempted to lift it too early, as it will break up.
3. When it is completely dry, peel it off the Teflon. One side will be shiny and smooth.

∧ Rock study pot with paste fabric and inkjet transfer paper. Enhanced by French knots.

Using heat to distress molding paste fabric

As always, when heating acrylic materials, it is advisable to protect yourself from fumes. Do work in a well-ventilated area and wear a mask. You could first distress the fabric and then work on it, or you could use a hot iron and prolonged heat to transfer inkjet transfer paper onto the fabric.

1. Place baking paper on an ironing board.
2. Put the paste fabric on this and cover with another sheet of baking paper.
3. Use a hot iron to iron over the fabric. Protect yourself from breathing in any possible fumes. Do not lift the baking paper until the fabric is cold.
4. The heat from the iron will have distorted and distressed the fabric. You can now use transfer techniques, paint, laminate, stamp or embroider the distressed paste fabric.

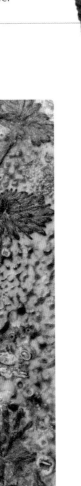

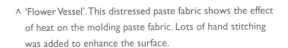

∧ 'Flower Vessel'. This distressed paste fabric shows the effect of heat on the molding paste fabric. Lots of hand stitching was added to enhance the surface.

Molding paste with Thermogauze

Another effect that can be achieved by using heat with molding paste is to apply it to vanishing muslin (Thermogauze). Vanishing muslin crumbles away with heat but the trick is not to use too much heat, so more fabric remains. Then you will have a delightfully distressed fabric contrasting with the heavier paste.

HERE'S HOW:

1. Working on baking paper, stencil some shapes onto the muslin, smoothing the material through it with a palette knife. Allow to dry and then place on a heatproof surface.
2. Working with good ventilation, use a heat tool sparingly until some of the muslin turns a darker shade.
3. Crumble it away, making sure that you leave enough to give a feathered edge.
4. Paint both paste and muslin – acrylic paint will lose the light feathery effect, so use silk or other runny paint.
5. When it is quite dry use a little gold wax or Markal on the paste.

> Light molding paste was applied to Thermogauze vanishing muslin through a stencil using a palette knife. It was zapped with a heat tool when dry and then painted. To make the sketchbook cover, the fragile pieces were hand stitched to a laminated silk paper background mounted on Vilene.

Casting with Golden Light Molding Paste

Some patience is required for this technique as it is necessary to wait until the paste is completely dry before removing it from your textured surface. You will need something with raised detail to obtain the cast 'fabric'. You can buy these textured items in the form of rubber stamps, rubber molding mats or plastic textured rubbing plates. Look for interesting surfaces to work on but do not use anything you would want to keep in pristine condition. Unmounted rubber stamps or texture mats work well as the rubber is pliable and you can peel it back when you want to remove the dry paste fabric.

Look for rubber stamps that are deeply etched and unmounted, as the paste fabric can be more easily removed from these.

If the rubber molding mat or stamp does not have deeply incised detail, it may be necessary to create a barrier to go between the textured item and the molding paste. This is so that the dry molding paste can be easily removed. The barrier that I use is Vaseline petroleum jelly. Vaseline works really well and it can be removed afterwards by gently washing the resulting paste 'fabric' and also the rubber molding mat. This means that the molding mat or stamp can still be used afterwards for different mixed media projects. Use your finger to apply the Vaseline to the textured surface and rub it into the crevices as far as you can. A thin smear is sufficient. A thick layer is unnecessary and will be more difficult to remove afterwards. Using Vaseline as a barrier can affect the paint finish (as described on page 50).

Use a plastic spatula to spread a thick layer of paste over the rubber stamp. Leave it to dry and then peel it off the rubber stamp.

The result is both robust and pliable. It can be applied to fabrics or used for brooches, medallions and bracelets.

Making your own moulding templates

Making your own template is easy and cheap but time-consuming. The bonus is that you will be in complete control of the resulting design and the jewellery will therefore be unique. Durable templates can be made by embossing copper relief foil. You will need a set of embossing tools, or an old ballpoint pen.

A4 sheets of copper relief foil are the cheapest and best foils to use for this technique. You can use designs from design source books or you can draw your own design.

HERE'S HOW:

1. Trace your design onto tracing paper.
2. Transfer the design to the copper foil. Work on an old glossy magazine and draw over the lines.
3. Remove the tracing paper and use embossing tools to raise the surface. Work on both sides of the foil.
4. Create a barrier by smearing Vaseline over the embossed copper.
5. Use a plastic spatula to spread molding paste over the copper. When the paste is dry, it should be easy to remove as the copper will peel back.

> Embossed copper relief foil used as a template for the pieces shown opposite.

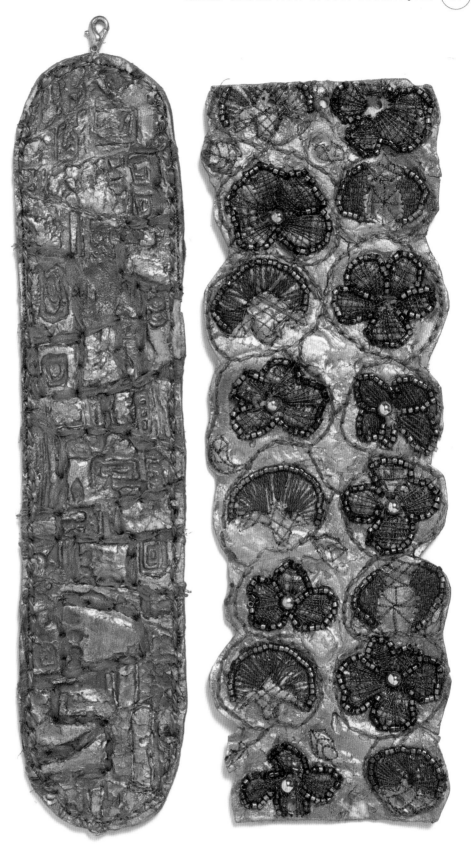

> Paste bangle made using an embossed copper
  template for the mould.
∧ Cast distressed paste bracelet made with a
  copper template.

Light Molding Paste for jewellery

Cast molding paste is perfect for making jewellery and we have lots of ideas on the following pages – try distressing, laminating and piping for some really different effects.

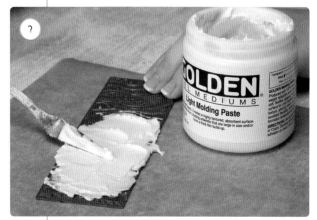

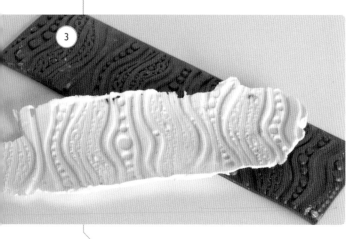

Bracelet

Make a paper pattern and ensure that the rubber stamp or texture mat is large enough to go around your wrist, or can be successfully joined.

HERE'S HOW:

1. Spread a thin layer of Vaseline over the rubber stamp. Use your finger to apply the Vaseline and do not apply thick layers.
2. Use a plastic spatula or your finger to spread the molding paste over the molding mat. Smooth out the layer of paste to ensure that an even layer of the mixture is spread. The rubber should not show through.
3. Leave the stamp to dry. When it is thoroughly dry, remove the impressed dry paste from the stamp.
4. Gently wash the 'fabric' or use a baby-wipe to remove the Vaseline. Any Vaseline that remains on the paste fabric will resist paint and will ultimately flake off. Therefore, unless you want to retain this characteristic, you should take care to remove all traces of the Vaseline.

ʌ Bangle with cast paste on a brass base.

Sanding back the layers

This is a great way to produce a distressed surface using the 'fabric' from the previous page. Layers of paint are wiped or lightly sanded back to reveal the colours below. To make the bracelet, stabilise the fabric with lightweight craft Vilene if necessary.

HERE'S HOW:

1. Cut the paste fabric to size, 20 x 5cm (8 x 2in.). Round the corners. Cut a piece of leather to this size.
2. Paint it with Old World Peasant paint by Earth Safe. This is a quick-drying paint which will give a solid bottom layer of colour.
3. When it is dry, use a paintbrush to push black acrylic paint all over the fabric, particularly into the crevices. Wipe off the excess surface paint with a baby-wipe, leaving the black paint in the crevices.
4. When the acrylic paint is dry, paint the rest of the fabric with paint of your choice. Paint the edges as well as the front and, when it is dry, sand it lightly to remove some of the paint.
5. Now hand embroider and bead as required.
6. Use 505 Spray glue to bond the embroidered fabric to the leather and cut around the shape before machine stitching around the edges. For a really tough finish, you could paint a sealant such as acrylic wax or Mod Podge over the surface.

YOU'LL NEED:

- Light Molding Paste
- Vaseline (optional)
- Texture mat
- Spatula
- Leather, suede or other suitable non-fraying fabric
- Paints of your choice
- Baby-wipes
- Acrylic wax or sealant such as Mod Podge
- 505 Spray glue
- Sanding block

Jagged edges

When creating the base layer of the textured molding paste, try fading out and making the edges thinner as you go. For jagged edges, use both hands to tear pieces off carefully. Colour and stitch the fabric as desired. Stem stitched organza ribbon was used for the necklace. As parts of the 'paste fabric' were deliberately made thin, a firm stabiliser is necessary to ensure that no further erosion will take place. The necklace and the bracelet illustrated were both bonded to leather.

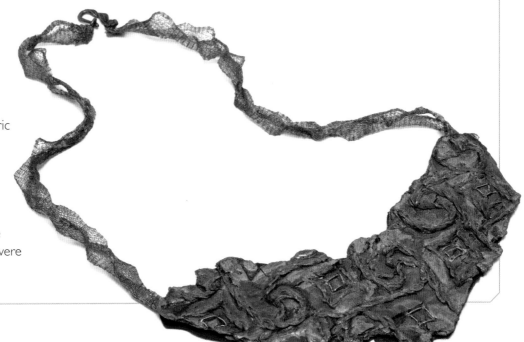

Cut-out shapes and embossing enamels

As molding paste can withstand a limited amount of heat from a heat tool, embossing enamels can be applied to add colour and interest.

Try layering different colours on selected areas. Remember the rule about stopping when you like what you see.

Shapes can be cut out from textured molding paste. These can be used for appliqué, brooches, buttons or standalone jewellery.

< Shapes cut out from paste fabric which was coloured and embossed.

∧ The technique used to make these attractive bracelets was to form mini 'bricks' from printed teabag paper which was laminated to paste rectangles.

Elastic bracelets

The back of these bracelets will require some thought and consideration. A fabric that does not fray is the best option. Buying leather off-cuts is not necessarily expensive and soft pliable leather is tactile.

The textured molding paste bricks should be about 0.5cm (¼ in.) thick. This will not only make them robust but it will also enable you to sew through the brick using elastic thread. Sew the backing to the bricks and then thread a large needle with strong elastic. Push the needle through one molding paste brick at a time and then thread on the bead or beads. You may find that the needle and thread will not pass through the bead. If this is the case then it usually works if you remove the needle and push the end of the elastic through the hole in the bead. Threading the needle to sew through the brick and then removing it to thread on the beads can be a little frustrating but this method works.

The bricks above were made on molding paste tiles that were laminated with printed teabag paper.

The bricks below were formed by setting molding paste over a deeply etched Stewart Gill stamp.

∨ Paste fabric bricks were formed over a deeply etched Stewart Gill stamp.

< For this necklace, beads made from dried, rolled rose petals were mixed with iced paste beads and medallions.

ᵛ This iced paste medallion is combined with stitched paper 'rocks' and purchased beads.

Icing tubes and molding paste

This technique opens up all sorts of possibilities and is great fun. The resulting shapes are easy to colour and stitch into. Filigree shapes or larger, more solid shapes can be piped. When they are coloured, they can be extensively stitched into and will not crumble. They can be used for bracelets, necklaces and rings.

Try combining the paste beads with bought beads or other handmade beads.

HERE'S HOW:

1. Place the icing nozzle in position in the icing tube.
2. Use the knife to place the molding paste in the icing tube.
3. Ice your design onto the baking paper or baking Teflon (you could make beads or buttons).
4. Leave it to dry.
5. Use paints of your choice to colour the resulting shapes. Sometimes it is advantageous to paint three colours onto the shape and, while the paint is still wet, rub it off with a baby-wipe.

YOU'LL NEED:
- Icing tube and nozzle
- Molding paste
- Baking paper
- Paints of your choice
- Plastic knife or spatula
- Baby-wipes

> Molding paste iced medallion with twisted Softsculpt band.

CHAPTER 4

DISTRESSING TECHNIQUES

Crackle paste

This is a great material for adding a textured, distressed finish. We've found the most reliable are made by Ranger – the Tim Holtz distress crackle pastes were used on items throughout this book. Some of the others tend to flake when used for mixed media work. However, do try whatever you've got in the cupboard first. The pastes can be bought already coloured or you can change the colour by painting over them. The resulting fabric can be moulded to form bracelets, or combined with other media to great effect.

Crackle pastes are fun and are easy to use. The crackle effect does not appear until the paste is completely dry – this can be speeded up with the use of a heat tool.

< Sketchbook cover based on rocks: crackle paint on kozo paper.

< Detail of piece shown on page 58 illustrating the fine crackle that can be achieved with crackle paints.

∧ Sketchbook with crackle paint experiments.

∨ Painted newspaper with crackle paint offers
  an unusual surface.

Crackle paste on paper

Try crackle paste on a paper background – just paint it on to give good coverage. The sample piece shown here was made like this:

HERE'S HOW:

1. Paint streaks of crackle paste onto printer-weight paper that has been lightly crumpled by scrunching into a ball and unwrapping. Allow to dry.
2. Dampen the areas between the streaks and tear away the paint-crackled areas.
3. Apply to a background of painted crumpled paper.
4. Use spray glue on the back of the paper to attach it to felt and then stitch by hand or machine. Strips of sheer fabric can be added before stitching.

You can see, right, the sketchbook pages that inspired this design.

∧ Sketchbook designs were developed from fossil fishes and used as a base for the textile above. Cut-out Grungepaper and gilded molding paste form the geometric shape on the left, which provides a contrast to the stitched and applied fish.

Crackle paste with Light Molding Paste

Allow the molding paste to dry before adding crackle paste. Some crackle pastes work better than others for wearable art.

HERE'S HOW:

1. Smear Vaseline over a rubber stamp.
2. Use a plastic spatula to apply molding paste over the stamp.
3. Wait until the paste is completely dry before removing it.
4. Use a baby-wipe to remove any traces of Vaseline. Traces of Vaseline will inhibit the successful adhering of the paint so, for a distressed surface, do not remove all traces.
5. Paint Tim Holtz distress crackle glaze paint on top of dry textured molding paste.

When it is dry, the crackle glaze can be painted and pieces can be chipped off to reveal distressed layers. A final coat of acrylic wax or a sealer such as Mod Podge or Jo Sonja's can be used if necessary.

∨ Icing tube paste beads are mixed with commercial beads and a distressed paste medallion which combines crackle paste with Light Molding Paste.

Stamping with crackle paste on kozo paper

It is possible to stamp with Tim Holtz crackle paint. You will get a distressed appearance because not all of the paste will be transferred to the paper or fabric. Use stamps that have deeply carved detail, such as some wooden stamps, or make your own from Funky Foam. Stamps made from Funky Foam will take on the shape but will not show up incised detail.

If you want neat edges for your jewellery or wearable art, try working on non-fraying fabrics such as textured mulberry paper, kozo paper, silk paper or Evolon. Textured kozo paper was used to cover the brass bangle featured opposite.

< Detail of the stamped kozo paper used for the bag and bangle.

HERE'S HOW:

To make the 'fabric' for the bangle illustrated, work like this:

1. Add texture by hand stitching thick threads or yarns in selected places. Running stitch was used here.
2. Seal the fabric or paper with Old World Peasant paint by Earth Safe. Apply a liberal coating so that it soaks into the paper or fabric and covers the stitches. This paint was used because it dries to leave a plasticised white coating, which adds to the strength of the paper. Alternatively, paint white gesso over the paper.
3. When the base coat of paint is dry, colour the fabric with paints of your choice. The kozo paper used to make this bangle was coloured by spraying burgundy Glimmer Mist over it. When this was dry, burgundy encaustic wax was ironed over the paper with an encaustic iron. Alternatively a travel iron without steam vents can be used to apply the encaustic wax. The wax will remain on the raised surfaces. Always work in a well-ventilated area and wear a mask when applying any form of heat.
4. Use a sanding block to sand the textured paper lightly and reveal the base coat. (Work outside and wear a mask.)
5. Paint acrylic wax over the paper to seal it.

∧ Stamped kozo paper on a brass bangle base.

6. The paper is now ready to receive the distress crackle paste. Old Paper distress crackle paste by Tim Holtz was used to stamp the flower design. This paint is quite thick and comes with a dedicated brush inside the bottle. Apply the thick paint over a stamp that has deeply carved detail. A wooden stamp was used here but you could make your own. Not all of the pattern will be transferred using this technique, and this works well for a distressed appearance. Wash the excess paint off your stamp immediately you have finished stamping, or try wiping it onto fabric or paper, which can be used for another project, before washing it.
7. Leave the crackle paint to dry. You can speed up the process by heating it with a heat tool.

< Stamped kozo paper bag with a twisted Softsculpt button.

Superior Texture Magic

Sometimes a more robust material is needed and the vessel, shown below, based on rock wall art, needed something to represent the texture of the rocky surface. Texture Magic was selected as the material to be used to make the vessel.

Texture Magic is a white fabric, which resembles dress-lining material. It shrinks by 30% when heat from a steam iron is held over it. To work with other fabrics, place them on top and then stitch. After stitching, distort with a steam iron as described below. Texture Magic also works well when mixed media is applied directly on top of it. inkAID is particularly good. It is not just paper that can be used in the printer.

Making the vessel

Prepare the image that is to be printed onto the fabric. The image used here is from a page in a sketchbook.

Because Texture Magic shrinks when heat is applied, it cannot be ironed onto freezer paper and then inkjet-printed. Simply attaching it untreated to a carrier sheet will not work either, as most printers will not accept it. The solution is first to paint a slightly larger than A4 sheet of Texture Magic with inkAID. This not only seals it but also makes the fabric firmer. When attached to computer paper with masking tape, my printer found it more acceptable. We use matt pre-coat inkAID to paint the surface. Work on baking paper as the fabric is porous and it will seep through to the other side.

WHEN IT IS DRY, WORK LIKE THIS:

1. Place the fabric right side up on a carrier sheet, cut it to size and bind the edges with masking tape. This will make it more user friendly in the printer and will also prevent any pieces of inkAID from flaking off and falling into the printer mechanism.
2. Print the image onto the fabric and then remove the masking tape.
3. Hand stitch or machine stitch the fabric.
4. Hold a steam iron over the back to activate the shrinking process.
5. Make the fabric into a vessel or object of your choice.

> Vessel based on a study of rocks. Inkjet-printed Texture Magic made a firm base for the vessel.

Adding fusible webbing

This vessel, based on tree and plant studies, has fusible webbing bonded to it to represent plant growth. Ironing fusible webbing over the distressed Texture Magic flattens the fabric a little and thus alters the extent of its peaks and troughs.

Use Texture Magic and inkAID as previously described.

HERE'S HOW:

1. Inkjet-print the fabric.
2. Stitch and then shrink the fabric.
3. Seal the front of the fabric with Shimmer Mod Podge. This leaves a golden appearance.
4. Blend Tim Holtz translucent alcohol inks over the fabric to achieve the desired colour.
5. Cover the fabric with black FuseFX or black Misty Fuse (both are fusible webbings). Protect the iron by placing baking paper over the fabric. Iron to bond the webbing. I used a very hot iron and pressed hard. This made the FuseFX bond really well and at the same time it flattened out the distressed Texture Magic.

< This piece was based on a study of tree bark. Inkjet-printed Texture Magic with black fusible webbing gives an excellent texture, closely resembling the original bark.

^ The inspiration for the book was this Batik Peacock panel on cotton, made by Xantha Hall. It was scanned and printed on Texture Magic to produce the book cover shown below.

Using the reverse side of printed Texture Magic

If you use the technique described on the previous pages and inkjet-print vibrant colours onto inkAID-painted Texture Magic, some of the colours will show through on the back. You can go on to exploit this technique to create another design.

This peacock design was inkjet-printed onto the Texture Magic.

HERE'S HOW:

1. First paint inkAID over the Texture Magic.
2. When it is dry, attach it to a carrier sheet with masking tape.
3. Inkjet-print your design. Use a design with vibrant colours. (You could always paint or stamp your design onto the inkAID painted surface as an alternative to inkjet printing.) I used the peacock painting, shown left.
4. Machine stitch and hand stitch into the fabric.
5. Shrink the fabric using the steam from an iron.
6. Now turn the fabric over and seal the back by painting Mod Podge sealer over it. Matt Mod Podge sealer was used here. This will stabilise the inkAID and leave a more plasticised surface. The back will now become the front.
7. Finally use Tim Holtz alcohol inks to colour the fabric. These inks are translucent so the colours from the inkjet printer still remain visible. We used Butterscotch, Denim and Bottle alcohol inks and blended them with the blending solution made by the same company. This changed the appearance quite dramatically.

^ Azurite rock vessel: Texture Magic, silk paper and smocking thread were
used for the vessel. The fabric has hand-made coloured crystals applied.

Texture Magic, silk paper and smocking thread

Both Texture Magic and Madeira smocking thread have shrinking properties. Used together on firmer fabrics, they distort and shrink in a pleasing way. We tried them on robust silk paper. The stone vessel was made as part of the rocks and stones project. An ongoing study of the malachite and azurite rocks found near Isobel's home in an old mining village led to the creation of this vessel.

IT WAS WORKED LIKE THIS:

1. Robust silk paper was made using one part acrylic gloss medium to four parts water.
2. Designated areas were coloured with heat-fixable paint.
3. When the paint was dry, the fabric was placed over Texture Magic.
4. With Madeira smocking thread in the bobbin and on the top, free machine embroidery was used to stitch into the layers.
5. Heat from a steam iron was used to activate the shrinking process.
6. Clear Opals Franklin embossing enamels were coloured by alcohol inks and by Adirondack spray paints – see below for the technique.
7. Acrylic wax was painted over the fabric in designated areas. The coloured crystals were sprinkled over the top and then a heat tool was used to activate the crystals.
8. Acrylic wax was painted over the top so that the piece was integrated.

Making your own coloured crystals

Making your own coloured crystals is an interesting technique which can be great fun. It is easy to make your own and you will be able to co-ordinate colours for a unique effect. We used Opals Franklin embossing enamels for this technique.

HERE'S HOW:

1. Place the required amount of clear Opals Franklin embossing enamels in an empty, clean ice-cream tub.
2. Have a small wooden stick like a toothpick handy, as you have to work quickly for the next stage.
3. Add colour by shaking small amounts of Tim Holtz alcohol inks into the tub.
4. Stir with the stick. Do not touch the crystals as they will colour your hands.
5. Paint acrylic wax over the fabric and while it is still wet sprinkle the coloured enamels over the fabric. Shake the excess off – back into the ice-cream tub.
6. Use a heat tool to activate the crystals. Care should be taken not to burn the base fabric.

CHAPTER 5

RECYCLE AND RE-USE

In this section we're really getting to grips with recycling. As you can see from this page, even the humble plastic bottle can become a treasured piece of jewellery, and these are lovely for gifts. Old wire is also good for bracelets, and old buttons can be recycled into 'pinwheels'.

Wrapped bottle bracelets

Bracelets can be cheaply made by recycling empty circular plastic bottles. Use scissors to cut out the shape. Start at the top and keep cutting around the bottle until you reach the bottom. The strip needs to be about 2cm (¾in.) wide. Don't worry if the edges are not straight. The finished width will probably be about 1cm (½in.) wide. You need this excess in order to trim the plastic strip to size.

For the ribbon-wrapped bracelet, above right, trim the plastic and then wrap the strip.

∧ Wrapped plastic with cast paste medallion.

The tape bracelet, left, should be made by leaving the plastic strip as it is and stitching the flat tape onto it. Only then should the plastic be cut to size.

Wrap or stitch the tape or ribbon to the plastic strip.

Add decoration of your choice.

For both bracelets, use the same tape or ribbon to secure the ends in one place – this neatens the bracelet and holds it in place.

< Bracelet made from water-bottle plastic with stitched tape and decorated with Mylar Shimmer Sheetz embossed fish.

Wrapped bottle bracelets with Light Molding Paste

This technique opens up all sorts of possibilities. In order to ensure that the bracelet remains easy to stitch, the plastic should first be wrapped with ribbon or tape.

HERE'S HOW:

1. Cut the plastic bottle to obtain the coils.
2. Wrap a piece of double-sided tape around one end. About 1cm (½in.) is sufficient.
3. Start by wrapping the ribbon onto the double-sided tape and continue to wrap until you reach the other end. Secure this end, also with double-sided tape. Leave about 10cm (4in.) of ribbon dangling and cut the ribbon so that there is a tail hanging. (Sari ribbon was used to wrap this plastic.)
4. Lightly cover both sides of the wrapped plastic with molding paste. I find it easier to work on baking paper. Also cover the strip that is hanging as this will be used to wrap round all of the coils when forming the bracelet. Leave the paste to dry.
5. Paint the paste with paints of your choice. Using more than one colour and blending the colours looks best. You could use a baby-wipe to blend the colours.
6. Decorate the plastic strip when the paint is dry. The bracelet shown here was wrapped with gold thread, overlapped in one direction. When you reach the other end, wrap the strip again, working in the other direction so that the threads cross. You can stitch into or bead the plastic strip. Stitching will be easy if you slide the needle through the molding paste and ribbon. Finally, make coils and secure them by wrapping the ribbon around and stitching it in place.

Λ Wrapped water-bottle plastic with ribbon and molding paste.

Wrapped wire with beads

Old wire can be wrapped with ribbon to make bracelets.

HERE'S HOW:

1. These bracelets need to slip over the wrist of the wearer and the best way to achieve the required shape and size is to experiment by wrapping the wire around different-sized circular containers until the correct size is found.

2. The wire can then be cut to size and straightened out. A straightened-out wire is easier to wrap and stitch into.

3. To wrap the wire, begin by winding a small piece of double-sided tape about 1 cm (½ in.) around one end. Bond the starting edge of the ribbon to this. As you will want to stitch into the ribbon, it's best if you do not use too much double-sided tape (difficult to stitch into and it makes the needle sticky). If you do have to stitch into this tape then the needle can be wiped with a baby-wipe.

4. Use double-sided tape at the end of the wire and, if you need to make a join, use the double-sided tape for it. When you get to the end, wrap the ribbon around all of the circles and secure it.

∧ Wrapped wire with coated paper leaves and iced molding paste beads.

∧ Wrapped wire with rose petal beads and iced molding paste beads.

Wrapped wire with transparent papers

Bought beads, mixed with shapes cut from transparent papers, decorate this bracelet. Try using pale colours to paint fragile papers such as teabag paper or bookbinder's tissue. You could use watercolour paints such as Twinkling H$_2$O. Alternatively you could use pale colours to marble the paper.

HERE'S HOW:

1. Use the method of your choice to marble the paper.
2. Paint acrylic wax or Mod Podge over the fragile papers. Work on baking paper and leave it on the paper to dry.
3. Iron clear encaustic wax over the paper.
4. Use a heat tool to re-heat the wax and sprinkle clear embossing powder such as Opals Franklin over the hot wax. Remember the safety precautions. Heat again with a heat tool to melt the embossing powder.
5. Cut or punch out shapes. Embroider the shapes. Buttonhole stitch, worked loosely around the edges, works well as both sides are visible through the transparent fabric. Treat the shapes with care. Once they are sewn to the bracelet, they will be serviceable.

∧ Wrapped wire with coated transparent papers and purchased beads.

Fishing wire and hot melt glue

An exciting chance encounter with a weedy sea dragon in Narooma, Australia, led Isobel to explore sketchbook work based on this wonderful creature. Initially, the sea dragon looked like a piece of moving seaweed and it was only on closer inspection that it became apparent that it was in fact an amazing sea creature.

Weedy sea dragon bracelet

HERE'S HOW:

1. A hot melt glue-gun was used to represent the sea dragon. Droplets of glue were squeezed onto baking paper.
2. When cold, these were coloured with alcohol ink.
3. Old fishing wire was used to replicate the tangled mass of seaweed. It too was coloured with green alcohol ink. Loose Irish crochet was made to form a bracelet.
4. The coloured glue 'sea creatures' were sewn onto the bracelet so that they formed a decorative edge. As the Irish crochet was loosely formed, the fishing wire stretched to enable the bracelet to go on the wrist. It springs back in place when it is being worn.

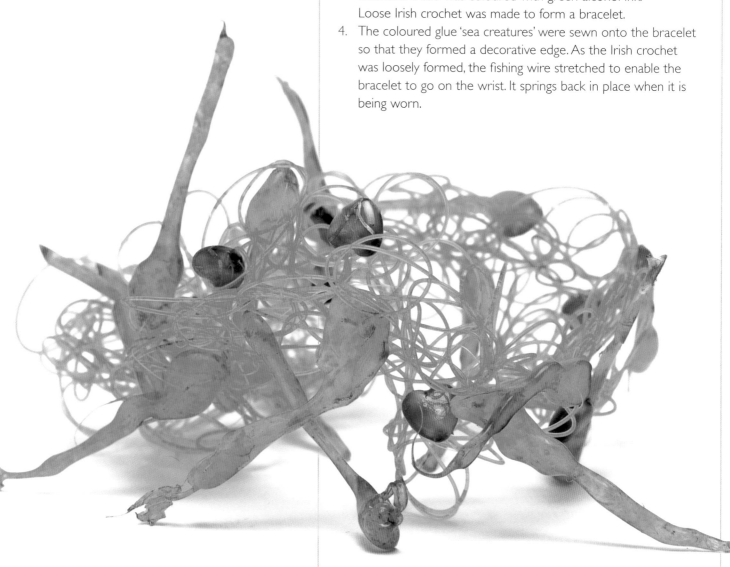

∧ Crocheted fishing wire, coloured with alcohol inks and glue-gun 'dragons'.

Necklace

The matching necklace was made in much the same way in that ribbon was loosely crocheted to form the base to go around the neck. The ribbon is soft and tactile and as such it is comfortable to wear. The baby sea dragons, made from glue, were sewn in place. The fastening catch at the back of the neckpiece was made from an iced molding paste bead.

Edwardian buttons

Bracelets, buttons, brooches, rings and pendants can all be made using the basic techniques for wrapped buttons.

Flat bases should be used to make them. The wrapped cords or ribbons need to be held in place by stitching them on the back. The addition of double-sided sticky tape is also advantageous.

∧ Heated Softsculpt was pressed into a wrapped button. Beads were added and were also used to join the buttons and make a bracelet.

HERE'S HOW:

1. Select a flat button with no raised areas, or a firm circular disc.
2. Wrap the button with ribbon, piping or yarn of your choice. You may find it easier to place double-sided tape on the back and attach the first threads to this. Begin by wrapping three threads in a vertical direction. (The number of threads you decide to wrap in each direction is dependent upon how large your circle is and how thick the yarn is.)
3. Change direction and wrap three threads horizontally. Secure the threads to hold them in place on the back by making a few stitches.
4. Wrap three threads in a diagonal direction and secure them.
5. Wrap three threads on the other diagonal and secure them.
6. Continue to wrap around until all of the gaps are filled.

You can leave the button as it is or you can alter it by adding beads or stitches. You can also change it by painting over the wrapped cords.

When completed, the button can be used as a mould by pressing heat-mouldable foam (Softsculpt) into the wrapped button. This makes a new button with a textured surface that can be stitched.

∧ Button made from used painted baking paper.

Edwardian pinwheel buttons

Home-made buttons were sometimes made simply from strips of fabric that were coiled to form a circle. They were stitched roughly on the back to hold the coils in place. Apart from making buttons, this technique can be used to make different types of jewellery and beads.

If you work on baking paper when you are using paint with a roller for another project, you will end up colouring the paper also. Don't throw this away as it can be used to make pinwheel decorations. Thick acrylic paints or thick heat-fixable paints work well for this technique.

To make it into jewellery, cut it into strips which are about 2.5cm (1in.) wide. Fold the paper strip once or twice and roll it to form a pinwheel button. Hold it in place with stitches on the back. Add beads and make it into the top of a ring, a medallion or a brooch.

∧ Collagraph plate used for the background print below.

∨ The background here is a series of pasta machine prints from the
plate above, collaged to form a larger piece. The circular net on
the plate fits well with the ammonite and fossil fish theme.

Re-using equipment

We've all got gadgets and gizmos tucked away at
the back of the cupboard. So how about trying a
liquidiser to distress some silk flowers, or a pasta
machine for making collagraphs?

Pasta machine collagraphs

Collagraphy is a printmaking technique that uses
collage to create the printing plate. You work
directly with your materials, which allows you
to explore and experiment, and the texture
obtained from such materials as scrim and lace
is amazing. To get good results, you do really
need a press – which is a big investment. A pasta
machine can be purchased quite cheaply and,
although small, the results can be built up into
bigger pieces. It is best to save it for printing and
not be tempted to make the family supper with
the studio machine.

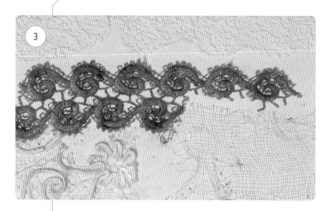

Jane Wild makes fantastic collagraphs.

HERE IS JANE'S METHOD:

1. Cut a small rectangle or square of mountboard to make a base. This must be narrower than the width of the rollers of the pasta machine.

2. Decide which materials you would like to work with. Use lace, scrim, cut card or paper, netting or anything weird and textural. Try to get a variety of textures and start cutting and tearing them into different shapes and sizes.

3. Begin attaching the textured pieces to the board with watered-down PVA glue or acrylic medium. Make sure that the highest point of the surface you create is no higher than two thicknesses of mountboard – otherwise you run the risk of tearing the paper. Leave the plate while the glue dries out completely – this may be overnight.

4. When the plate is completely dry, coat it back, front and sides with acrylic gel or PVA glue thinned with water. When dry, apply another coat and leave to dry again. This will strengthen and protect the plate.

5. Finally coat the plate back, front and sides with button polish or shellac and leave overnight to harden.

6. Before you start printing, cut your paper to size. Allow enough paper for a small border around the print but make sure it is slightly narrower than the width of the pasta machine rollers.

7. Leave the paper to soak in a container of water for at least ten minutes and then place it between two sheets of blotting paper to remove the excess water. It should be damp, not wet.

8. Cut a piece of felt or wool slightly narrower than the width of the rollers and slightly longer than your longest plate. Before you print with ink, you can make an embossed or blind print by running the plate and a piece of paper through the pasta machine. Place the piece of felt on your work surface, cover the felt with a piece of damp paper and then place the plate face down on the paper. Roll through the pasta machine as in step 11.

9. Squeeze out some acrylic printing ink or acrylic paint onto a piece of plastic or glass. The acrylic paint could be mixed with Daler-Rowney acrylic printing medium to a fairly runny consistency. Tear small pieces of mountboard to spread the paint onto the plate and use a brush to work it into the grooves and textured areas.

10. Use a wad of muslin or paper towel to wipe the ink from the surface of the plate. This seems wasteful but it is essential. Then prepare as in step 8.

11. With the pasta machine firmly attached to the work surface and the rollers at the widest setting, start to feed the felt, paper and plate between the rollers. This is quite tricky and you have to be ready to encourage the plate forward slightly as it rolls through or it will hit the base of the machine. Test it out first with a scrap of mountboard to get the idea. Keep winding the handle smoothly.

∧ Collagraphs by Jane Wild, made using the
plate shown top right. Note the detail that
can be achieved.

^ Bag and bracelet made from silk paper with
stamped crackle paint. Blasted and blitzed flowers
were applied with non-blitzed flower shapes used
to edge the top of the bag.

Blasted and blitzed silk paper flowers from the liquidiser

Throwing silk felted flowers into a blender is very liberating. The results are unpredictable and it can be an exciting adventure. Experimenting with various types of felt and silk paper made with different strengths of glue produces very different results, as does using silk paper with woven fabrics as opposed to felts.

HERE'S HOW:

1. Begin by making the silk paper or use up scraps of silk paper left over from other projects. I prefer silk paper made from one teaspoon of Jo Sonja's fabric medium to eight teaspoons of water. The fibres hold together but the paper remains soft to the touch.
2. Place the silk paper over the wool batts. Soft wool batts that are ready to be felted work best for this technique.
3. Use a needle felting machine (embellisher) to join the two layers or use a felting punch, by hand.
4. Place the joined layers on the flat bed of the sewing machine and use free embroidery to loosely embroider the outline of a flower.
5. Cut out the flower.
6. Place one flower at a time in the blender and blitz until ready. Watch carefully to see how much you want to distress it. Wear a mask so that you do not inhale any of the wool or fluff that will be created. Watch and listen, as sometimes the sewing machine thread gets tangled on the blades. Stop the machine immediately should this happen. These are usually the best distorted flowers.
7. Appliqué the blasted flowers to fabric of your choice. They could be used for many applications.

Try blasting and blitzing other shapes in the blender and experiment with different needle-felted fabrics.

> Detail of blasted flowers which have
  been in the blender.

YOU'LL NEED:

- Needle felting machine or hand punch
- Sewing machine
- Silk paper as described
- Wool batts *
- Machine embroidery thread
- Scissors
- Liquidiser or blender
- Mask (optional)

* Wool batts from Australia or Norway work best as they are very soft. Otherwise use the softest wool that you can find.

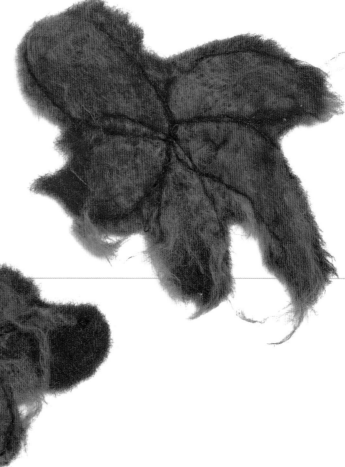

Using blitzed flowers as motifs

Here is an idea for using the liquidiser flowers with a
background built up from techniques used in the book.

BACKGROUND

Work on lightweight Vilene.

1. Place Vilene over tree bark or dried
   prickly pear cactus skeleton.
2. Rub with different-coloured Markal oil
   sticks and leave to dry.
3. Paint background with Twinkling H_2O
   paints (paint the back, not the front).
4. Paint transparent crackling paint
   (by Croco) over the fabric.
5. Apply the blasted flowers.

> Detail of the background. Lightweight craft
  Vilene with mixed media applied.

∨ Detail of flowers not put in the blender.

Insect netting

The floral design shown here is made from insect netting, paper and Light Molding Paste.

WORK LIKE THIS:

1. Place the netting on commercial paper and apply molding paste through a stencil.
2. Add distress crackle paste in some areas.
3. When dry, give it a coat of bronzing powder mixed with acrylic wax. A little rust patination fluid could be added on top.
4. For the flowers, sandwich fruit insect netting between two sheets of sheer fabric and stitch. Cut out shapes and blast with a heat tool. (You really do have to wear a respirator and work in a well-ventilated area as there are fumes when you heat the netting.)
5. Finally, distress the shapes and fray the edges by putting them in the blender.

< Detail of book cover with kozo paper which had molding paste applied through a stencil. Insect netting flowers with beaded centres were applied.

We do hope you've enjoyed working through some of the ideas in this book and that you will carry on with the experiments. The Golden Rule is ... there are no rules! So adapt our ideas to suit the way that you work and, most of all, have fun.

Suppliers

UK

21st Century Yarns
Good selection of yarns, silk fibres, dyed scrim and felt
Unit 18, Langston Priory Workshops
Kingham
Oxon OX7 6UP
yarns21stcentury@aol.com

Ario
Stewart Gill products, sealants, Evolon, Golden Molding Paste & Digital Ground, Distress Crackle Paint, mixed media products
5 Pengry Road
Loughor
Swansea SA4 6PH
fiona@ario.co.uk

Art Van Go
FuseFX, inkAID, most mixed media products, sealants
1 Stevenage Road
Knebworth
Herts SG3 6AN
art@artvango.co.uk

Barnyarns
Threads, sewing accessories, Texture Magic
Canal Wharf
Bondgate Green
Ripon
North Yorks HG4 1AQ
www.barnyarns.co.uk

Crafty Notions
Opals Franklin enamels, stencils and molding mats
Unit 2, Jessop Way
Newark NG24 2ER
www.craftynotions.com

Isobel Hall
Teabag paper, encaustic wax
isobelhall@gmail.com

Jennifer Gail Threads
Space-dyed threads and fabrics (see picture right)
The Garden Studio
10 Central Avenue, Poole
Dorset BH12 2EW
jenny@jgthreads.com

L.B. Crafts
Earth Safe paints, transparent crackling paint
6 Rose Court
Market Place
Olney MK46 4BY
shop@lbcrafts.com

Nid-noi.com
Evolon, transfer foil, craft and pelmet Vilene
126 Norwich Drive
Brighton BN2 4LL
info@nid-noi.com

Norwegian Wool UK
Wool batts
2 Beckside, Caton
Lancaster LA2 9RN
maggy@norwegianwool.co.uk

Nostalgia
Brass bangles and findings
147A Nottingham Road
Eastwood
Nottingham NG16 3GJ
info@Nostalgiaribbon.com

Oliver Twists
Cocoon strippings, silk filament and fibres, threads, tubular ribbon, metal shim
22 Phoenix Road
Crowther, Washington
Tyne and Wear NE38 0AD
olivertwistsretail@fsmail.net

Texere Yarns
Cocoon strippings, silk fibres
College Road
Barkerend Road
Bradford BD1 4AV
info@texere.co.uk

Winifred Cottage
Flat knitting tape, yarns, Tissutex, craft and pelmet Vilene, 505 Spray glue
17 Elms Road
Fleet
Hants GU51 3EG
sales@winifredcottage.co,uk

USA

Golden Artist Colors, Inc.
Light Molding Paste, Digital Ground, all Golden products
188 Bell Road
New Berlin, NY 13411-9527
www.goldenpaints.com

Joggles
Jo Sonja's textile medium, Mod Podge, silk cocoons and fibres, and lots more
Joggles.com, LLC
1454 Main Street Unit 30
West Warwick, RI 02893-3883
www.joggles.com

Soft Expressions
Texture Magic, Grungeboard
1230 N. Jefferson Street, Suite M
Anaheim, CA 92807
www.softexpressions.com

AUSTRALIA

The Thread Studio
Texture Magic, Grungeboard, inkAID, Evolon, soft wool batts, most items
6 Smith Street
Perth WA 6000
Australia
mail@thethreadstudio.com